A Definitive Guide on Where to Go and Things to Do

Homer, Alaska
Travel Guide
2023

Curtis Kerr

Table of Contents

INTRODUCTION

Welcome to Homer, Alaska

Homer, which is perched on the brink of Kachemak Bay, is a symbol of Alaska's unadulterated beauty. This thriving seaside community is a mesmerizing fusion of the tenacious spirit of its inhabitants, creative expression, and the glories of nature.

Prepare to enter a world where adventure and calm go hand in hand as you go to Homer, where snow-capped mountains meet the glistening sea.

Each moment appeared to stand still amid the untamed beauty of Homer, Alaska. As I stood on the pebbled coast and admired Kachemak Bay's emerald vastness, the salty wind pulled at my hair.

The mountains and the sea were in a beautiful embrace in a landscape that had been drawn by nature.

I was intrigued by the local art scene while I was strolling through the busy streets of this seaside town. The bright brushstrokes of paint caught the character of a town where fishermen and dreamers coexisted, while the galleries seemed to whisper sea tales. Homeric symphonies were created as the aroma of just-caught fish mixed with the sounds of street musicians drifted from outdoor eateries.

I came to understand that this was a magical site when the sun fell below the horizon, illuminating the Homer Spit with a warm golden light. There was a clear connection between the people, the land, and the sea. I enjoyed outdoor activities, the richness of the regional food, and the friendliness of the locals in the days that followed.

Homer was more than simply a place to go; it was a call to embrace the spirit of discovery and immerse oneself in its natural beauties. I had a feeling of belonging to a universe where time was defined by the ebb and flow of the tide as I explored new layers of its beauty every day.

A stunning view that runs from the untamed seashore to the far-off peaks of the Kenai Mountains will welcome you as soon as you enter Homer. The long, thin strip of land known as the Spit, which protrudes into the bay, extends its welcoming arms to you. Get ready to be mesmerized by the rhythmic melody of the seagulls above and the salty flavor of the sea wind.

Whether you're an experienced fisherman or a first-time visitor, the people in Homer will make you feel like a member of the family, reflecting the town's moniker, the "Halibut Fishing Capital of the World." The streets are lined with tempting cafes, adorable shops, and attractive art galleries, all of which invite you to stroll about at your speed.

1.2 Why Travel to Homer?

Homer is more than simply a place to go; it's an experience that goes above and beyond the norm. The town's unmatched environment offers a blank slate for a myriad of experiences.

Discover the splendor of Kachemak Bay State Park, where kayaks float on crystal-clear waterways and hiking routes weave through lush woodlands. Join trips that focus on wildlife watching to see bald eagles soar above, whales breach, and bears amble down the coast.

Homer is a creative resource for those who like the arts. While cultural institutions like the Pratt Museum provide insights into the region's rich history, its galleries include artwork that perfectly captures the spirit of

Alaska's environment. Enjoy farm-to-table delicacies and freshly caught seafood while indulging in the local culinary scene.

Homer invites you to enter a world where the magnificence of nature coexists with human creativity, whether you're looking for outdoor thrills, creative inspiration, or just a simple vacation from the ordinary. Join us as we discover the beauties of this seaside paradise, where every minute offers the chance to create priceless memories.

2. How to Get to Homer

2.1 Transportation Alternatives

Even though Homer is hidden away in the wild beauty of Alaska, getting here is simpler than you may imagine. There are many ways to get to this seaside treasure:

a. By Air: You may link to significant cities in Alaska and beyond through scheduled and charter flights from the Homer Airport (HOM). Regular service from airlines like Alaska Airlines and Ravn Alaska guarantees a hassle-free trip to and from Homer.

b. By Road: The Sterling Highway (Alaska Path 1) is your path to Homer if you're ready for a beautiful road journey. The stunning scenery along this roadway provides possibilities for sightseeing and photography.

c. By ferry: The Homer Ferry Terminal is a part of the Alaska Marine Highway System, which links the town to other coastal settlements and even to the rest of North America. This is a wonderful way to see the stunning Alaskan shoreline from the boat.

2.2 Weather and the Best Times to Travel

Visiting Homer at the ideal time may substantially improve your experience. Because of its seaside position, the town has pleasant summers and somewhat mild winters:

Summer (June to August): With good reason, this is the busiest travel period. With typical temperatures ranging from 50 to 65°F (10 to 18°C), the weather is at its finest. There are many opportunities for outdoor exploration and recreation because of the long daylight hours, including hiking, kayaking, fishing, and animal observation.

Fall (September to October): Although there are fewer visitors throughout the fall, the breathtaking scenery is still there. The fauna is still active, and the vegetation takes on bright colors. Starting to cool down are temperatures between 40 and 55°F (4 and 13°C).

Winter (November to February): Homer is more tranquil throughout the winter. Despite lows of 20 to 30°F (-6 to -1°C), the town's charm is unaffected. Cross-country skiing, snowshoeing, and even ice fishing are all popular winter activities.

Spring (March to May): Homer wakes to longer days and the prospect of regeneration as winter draws to a close. The typical temperature is between 0 and 45°F (-30 to -7°C). As migrating birds arrive back in the region in the spring, it's a terrific time to go bird-watching.

3. Homer's Accommodation Options

Homer has a selection of lodging choices to fit any traveler's needs and price range. You'll discover the ideal location to unwind and recharge, whether you're looking for a private getaway, a waterfront view, or a connection to nature.

3.1 Hotel and Lodges

The hotels and lodges in Homer provide convenience and comfort, sometimes with breathtaking views of the mountains or the sea. Here are a few illustrations:

a. The Land's End Resort is perched at the extremity of the Homer Spit and provides cozy rooms and suites with beautiful views of Kachemak Bay and the surrounding mountains. A restaurant, a bar, and event rooms are also available at the resort.

b. Located in the center of Homer's downtown, the Best Western Bidarka Inn provides quick access to the area's attractions. The well-appointed accommodations, free breakfast, and proximity to dining establishments and art galleries are all available to guests.

c. Homer Inn & Spa is a boutique hotel renowned for its tranquil ambiance. It provides opulent rooms and suites, some of which include soaking tubs and private balconies. A variety of treatments are available at the on-site spa to improve relaxation.

3.2 Vacation Rentals

Vacation rentals provide you the conveniences of home while letting you live like a local for those looking for a more genuine experience. Think about these choices:

a. Seaside homes: A calm haven is offered by the charming homes along the seashore. Enjoy a private terrace while taking in the sound of the surf, cooking in fully furnished kitchens, and relaxing.

b. Mountain View cottages: These tiny cottages are tucked away in the foothills of the Kenai Mountains and provide breathtaking views. Take in the peacefulness of the outdoors yet just a short drive from town.

c. Retreats into the arts: Many artists in Homer rent out their studios or cottages, offering a distinctive vacation amid artistic inspiration. These vacation accommodations often include local artwork and provide a unique touch.

3.3 Campsites

Homer's campsites provide a real Alaskan experience for travelers who wish to be close to nature:

a. Baycrest RV Park is situated on cliffs overlooking Kachemak Bay and has full-service RV sites. Enjoy contemporary facilities, expansive views, and quick access to trails.

b. Ohlson Mountain campsite: This modest campsite in a woodland offers tent pitches. For individuals who prefer to unplug and spend time in nature, it's a fantastic alternative.

c. Rustic Cabins: A few parks have inexpensive cabins that give shelter without compromising the camping experience. These cottages often feature modest facilities and wood-burning fireplaces.

Your time in Homer will be as memorable as the location itself, whether you like the comfort of a hotel, the intimacy of a vacation home, or the rustic appeal of camping.

4. Exploring Nature

Experience Homer's natural splendors firsthand by immersing yourself in it. Homer provides a wide range of possibilities to engage with nature, from pure wilderness to fascinating displays.

4.1 Kachemak Bay State Park

Kachemak Bay State Park, with its over 400,000 acres of untamed land, is a paradise for outdoor enthusiasts. This park has something for everyone, whether you're a seasoned hiker, a wildlife enthusiast, or just looking for peace:

a. Paths: There is a vast network of paths in the park that go through woodlands, meadows, and along the seashore. A well-liked alternative that provides breathtaking views of glaciers and alpine vistas is the Grewingk Glacier Lake Trail.

b. Kayaking: Set off on a kayaking expedition to discover the bay's secluded coves and beaches. Watch out for the seals, porpoises, and otters that call these waters home.

c. Camping: For individuals who want to spend the night completely alone in the bush, backcountry camping permits are available. Imagine waking up to a spruce tree smell and the sounds of nature.

4.2 Homer Spit Beaches

There are numerous beautiful beaches along the Homer Spit, a long and narrow stretch of land projecting into the sea. Each offers a distinctive viewpoint on Homer's coastline beauty:

a. Bishops Beach is a kid- and family-friendly location with tidepools to explore. The mountains across the water may be seen when you wander or beach comb there.

b. Mariner Park Beach: This beach is great for relaxing since it has picnic spaces and views of Kachemak Bay and the Spit. Kayakers often use it as a launch point.

c. Mud Bay is a tranquil beach well-known for its potential for birding. You may take a stroll outside at low tide to see the many bird species that inhabit this region.

4.3 Pratt Museum and Botanical Gardens

The Pratt Museum and Botanical Gardens are essential stops for anybody looking to learn more about Homer's natural history and cultural heritage:

a. Visit the Pratt Museum to immerse yourself in the displays that illustrate the area's rich history, from early settlers' daily lives to Native Alaskan culture. The museum has fascinating exhibits on animals, marine life, and the changing environment.

b. Botanical Gardens: The botanical gardens, which are next to the Pratt Museum, include native plants and vegetation from Alaska. Leisurely wander around themed gardens and take in the displays.

c. Exploring the outdoors in Homer is about more than just taking in the view; it's about getting to know the land, the sea, and the history that makes this extraordinary location. Every experience will give you a greater respect for nature, whether you choose to explore the trails of Kachemak Bay State Park, unwind on the beaches of the Homer Spit, or explore the exhibits at the Pratt Museum.

5. Outdoor Activities

The stunning natural surroundings of Homer provide the ideal setting for outdoor enthusiasts to partake in a range of thrilling activities. The town provides outdoor activities for every interest and ability level, whether you're an experienced explorer or a beginner.

5.1 Fishing Charters

Fishing charters are a must-do activity for anybody looking for an angling experience, and Homer's status as the "Halibut Fishing Capital of the World" is well-deserved:

a. Fishing for halibut: Take part in a fishing excursion to try your luck at landing the fabled halibut. These excursions provide everything you want, including fishing equipment and knowledgeable instruction, guaranteeing a wonderful day on the lake.

b. Fish for several types of salmon, including king salmon, silver salmon, and sockeye salmon, depending on the time of year. Catching a strong salmon is an exhilarating experience unlike any other.

5.2 Kayaking and Canoeing

Homer is a kayaker's heaven due to its tranquil seas and beautiful coasts. Pass past calm bays, scenic inlets, and secret coves as you paddle:

a. Kayaking at Kachemak Bay: Paddle around the waters of this state park while seeing marine species including otters, seals, and porpoises. The ecology may be better understood with guided excursions, which also provide a secure and educational environment.

b. Gull Island Paddle: Visit the seabird rookery on Gull Island to see thousands of birds in their natural environment. The puffins, kittiwakes, and cormorants that live on the island put up an amazing show.

5.3 Hiking Trails

Numerous hiking routes for hikers of all skill levels are available in Homer's varied scenery. Get your hiking boots on and discover the stunning Alaskan wilderness:

a. The moderate Bishop's Beach to Grace Ridge Trail provides breathtaking views of the Spit, Kachemak Bay, and the nearby mountains. It's a fantastic choice for a day trek.

b. Suitable for families, the Diamond Creek Trail leads to a pebble beach where beachcombing is encouraged. Along the trip, keep a look out for birds and marine life.

c. For those looking for a challenge, the Glacier Lake Trail leads to the picturesque Glacier

Lake, which is ringed by craggy rocks and, during certain times of the year, icebergs.

The outdoor activities in Homer are sure to leave you with lifelong memories of adventure and connection with nature, from the rush of catching a halibut to the peace of kayaking on the bay, and from the breathtaking panoramas on hiking trails to the delight of watching animals.

6. Wildlife Viewing in Homer

Homer's abundant biodiversity and distinctive coastline setting provide unrivaled possibilities to see magnificent wildlife in its native settings. These wildlife-watching opportunities will leave you wondering whether you're an enthusiastic birdwatcher, a marine mammal fanatic, or just inquisitive about Alaska's renowned critters.

6.1 Birding and Bald Eagles

With so many migrating birds and permanent birds, Homer is a sanctuary for bird enthusiasts:

a. Bald Eagles: Behold the magnificent bald eagles that reside in Homer. These majestic raptors may be seen hunting and soaring above the Homer Spit and neighboring estuaries.

b. Join guided birding trips at Kachemak Bay to learn about the many bird habitats there. Discover puffins, seabirds, and other bird species against the breathtaking bay and mountain background.

6.2 Whale Watching

Marine animals frequent the coastal seas of Homer, where there are exceptional possibilities to see them up close:

a. Observe humpback whales breaching and feeding in the bay for an unforgettable sight. Expert commentary and the opportunity to see these gentle giants in action are provided by guided whale-watching cruises.

b. Watching orcas: Orcas that travel often visit the seas around Homer. The great variety of marine life in the region is shown by seeing these sleek predators, which is an exhilarating experience.

6.3 Bears Viewing Tours

Take a bear-watching excursion for an exciting experience with Alaska's famous bears:

a. While not located in Homer itself, organized trips from Homer to Katmai National Park provide the chance to see bears harvesting salmon in their natural environment. It's an amazing display of nature.

b. Kachemak Bay Bear Tours: A few of these excursions take you to the wild, untouched areas of Kachemak Bay where you may see bears playing and feeding along the coast.

Homer's encounters with animals provide a window into the complex ecosystems of Alaska's coast. Each encounter gets you closer to the raw beauty of the natural world, whether you are enthralled by the majestic flight of eagles, the magnificent breaches of whales, or the mesmerizing presence of bears.

7. Homer's Culture and the Arts

As compelling as its natural beauty is, Homer's thriving arts and culture scene. Discover the creative energy that makes this city special, from galleries that feature local talent to historic sites that narrate the town's history.

7.1 Homer Galleries of Art

Visit the galleries to peruse the creations of regional artists and uncover the essence of Homer's creative expression:

a. Fireweed Gallery: Featuring a wide variety of artistic mediums, Fireweed Gallery offers anything from ceramics and jewelry to paintings and sculptures, all made by skilled Alaskan artists.

b. Ptarmigan Arts is an artist-owned cooperative gallery that displays a variety of top-notch works of art, such as paintings, photographs, ceramics, and more. It's a great location to purchase unique gifts to take home.

On the Homer Spit, the Art Shop Gallery is home to an extraordinary collection of works of art that beautifully depict the local fauna, landscapes, and cultures.

7.2 Bunnell Street Arts Center

The Bunnell Street Arts Center, a center for creativity and involvement in the community, is at the center of Homer's cultural scene:

a. Exhibits: The center holds revolving exhibits that highlight modern art in a variety of media and provide both homegrown and outside artists a stage on which to express their viewpoints.

b. Workshops and Events: The Bunnell Street Arts Center provides workshops, courses, and events that promote the growth of creative horizons and abilities. There is something for everyone, from painting to printing.

c. Residence Program for Artists: The center sponsors artists via its residence program, which enables them to become fully immersed in Homer's setting and culture while producing new works.

7.3 Salty Dawg Saloon

The Salty Dawg Saloon is a unique and well-known landmark where you may learn about local history and culture:

a. A special ambiance can be found inside the Salty Dawg Saloon, which has walls covered with hundreds of dollar notes that have been autographed by customers. Enjoy the relaxed atmosphere and friendly atmosphere.

b. Live Music: The saloon often holds live music events, giving patrons a chance to support local artists and mingle with the neighborhood.

c. Homer's maritime history is honored by the saloon, which is housed in a historic structure and offers a wholly genuine Alaskan experience.

Homer's artistic and cultural sites provide your trip richness and character, whether you want to enjoy works of visual art or immerse yourself in local history. You'll find a rich tapestry of creation that captures the essence of the town whether you're browsing galleries, taking part in seminars, or relaxing in a vintage saloon.

8. Dining & Cuisine in Homer

The culinary scene in Homer is a lovely blend of local cuisines, fresh fish, and a welcoming sense of community. Your taste senses are in for a treat, from feasting on freshly caught seafood to appreciating the creativity of local chefs.

8.1 Fresh Seafood Restaurants

Because of Homer's closeness to the sea, you can eat fish that is as fresh as it gets:

a. The well-known seafood restaurant Captain Patties Fish House serves a variety of meals, including fish and chips and seafood chowder, all of which are produced using ingredients that are acquired locally.

b. The Chart Room is a restaurant with breathtaking views of the Homer Spit and a varied seafood-focused cuisine. Make sure to sample meals like salmon burgers and tacos with halibut.

c. Fresh Catch Café: True to its name, Fresh Catch Café specializes in offering only the finest seafood. They offer meals like pan-seared scallops and seafood curry on their inventive menu.

8.2 Local Eateries

Visit the neighborhood restaurants in Homer to experience the town's distinctive cuisine:

a. A well-known bakery serving up freshly baked products, soups, and sandwiches is called Two Sisters Bakery. Enjoy a warm setting and a selection of vegetarian dishes.

b. Café Cups is a delightful café that emphasizes comfort meals and healthy products. Everything from breakfast classics to filling lunches may be found on their menu.

c. La Baleine Café is renowned for its distinctive and diverse menu, which features food with French, Mediterranean, and Asian influences.

8.3 Farmers' Markets

Visit the farmers' markets in Homer to get fully immersed in the community's culinary tradition:

a. Homer Farmers' Market: Open every Wednesday and Saturday, this market offers artisanal items, crafts, and live music in addition to fresh food. It's a terrific location to get to know residents and get a feel for the neighborhood.

b. Homer Spit Farmers' Market: If you're visiting the Spit during the summer weekends, don't miss this market. It provides a range of goods, including handmade trinkets and fresh fruit.

c. Homer Winter Market: Open on a limited schedule from October to May, the winter market offers a wealth of locally produced goods even during the colder months.

The culinary scene in Homer allows you to indulge in regional cuisines, from the sea's abundance to the inventiveness of neighborhood chefs. Your gastronomic experience in Homer will be a real expression of the town's culture and sense of community, whether you're indulging in seafood specialties, discovering local cafes, or meeting local producers at farmers' markets.

9. Day Trips and Excursions from Homer

While there are many things to do in Homer, you may discover even more of the breathtaking scenery and distinctive towns that make up this Alaskan treasure by taking day excursions to adjacent locations.

9.1 Halibut Cove

A visit to Halibut Cove for the day is a voyage into a remote haven of peace, nature, and art:

a. Take a scenic boat ride by boarding a ferry or water taxi to go to Halibut Cove. Awe-inspiring vistas of the bay, mountains, and marine life may be seen just from the ride itself.

b. Explore the local art culture at the distinctive Halibut Cove Art Gallery, which features pieces by both Alaskan and foreign artists.

c. Walk down the boardwalk as it snakes into the cove, past cute cottages, art galleries, and the famed Saltry Restaurant.

9.2 Seldovia Village

Learn about the charm of Seldovia Village, which is reachable by boat or ferry, to get a feel for Alaskan small-town life:

a. Seldovia port: Enjoy the sights of boats bobbing in the sea as you stroll around the port. Visit neighborhood stores and restaurants, such as the Seldovia Boardwalk Hotel.

b. Seldovia Museum: The Seldovia Museum has a remarkable collection of artifacts and displays that will help you learn more about the history of the community and its indigenous cultures.

c. Outdoor Adventures: Take part in outdoor pursuits like hiking, beachcombing, and kayaking while taking in the stunning coastal scenery of Seldovia.

9.3 Glacier Cruises

Take a glacier tour for an adventure you won't soon forget:

a. Embark on a cruise to see the glaciers, fjords, and wildlife of Kachemak Bay. Watch out for seals, otters, and sometimes even whales.

b. Some cruises stop in the Alaska Maritime National Wildlife Refuge, where you may see seabird colonies and the breathtaking island vistas that make up the refuge.

c. Glacier Sightseeing: Be in awe of the majestic glaciers that often calve, sending chunks of ice cascading into the water. The noises and images of moving glaciers are utterly captivating.

You may extend your Alaskan vacation by visiting these day trip locations from Homer, which look at local culture, beautiful scenery, and the mystique of glaciers. Each excursion promises to offer something special to your trip to Homer, whether you choose to see the creative sanctuary of Halibut Cove, savor the elegance of Seldovia Village, or go on a glacier cruise.

10. Events and Festivals

Homer's events and festivals are a great opportunity to get to know the community, appreciate local culture, and have interesting experiences. Here are some noteworthy occurrences together with their associated dates:

10.1 Homer Winter Carnival

Date: Typically occurring in February

The Homer Winter Carnival is a vibrant festival of wintertime pleasure and neighborhood pride. This multi-day celebration includes events including competitions for best snow sculptures, talent performances, parades, and winter sports. Celebrate the Alaskan winter in a joyful setting that will warm your soul.

10.2 Kachemak Bay Writers' Conference

Date: Typically in June

The Kachemak Bay Writers' Conference is a highlight of the year for book lovers and budding authors. For seminars, readings, and conversations, this gathering of distinguished authors, poets, and literary experts takes place. It's a rare chance to immerse oneself in the universe of language and narrative.

10.3 Summer Programs at the Pratt Museum

Dates: All through the summer

The Pratt Museum provides a range of interesting summer events that give insights into the people, places, and cultures of the area. These events, which range from led hikes and presentations to workshops and exhibits, provide a better knowledge of Alaskan culture.

Attending these activities in Homer not only ups the thrill factor of your vacation but also gives you the chance to meet people, get local knowledge, and make long-lasting memories of your stay in this alluring seaside town. As dates might change from year to year, be sure to check for the most recent information while making travel plans.

11. Useful Travel Information

11.1 Navigation and Maps

a. Offline Maps: Before your vacation, get offline maps of Homer and the neighborhood. If you're traveling through places with spotty cell coverage, this may be extremely useful.

b. Local guides are available in the form of printed maps and brochures at tourist centers or your lodging. These sites often contain attractions, hiking routes, and helpful data.

11.2 Communication and Language Tips

Widespread Use of English: Homer's native tongue is English. Travelers can communicate with people and service providers easily since the majority speak English well.

11.3 Health and Safety Tips

a. Animals Safety: Be mindful of the possibility of coming into contact with animals whether hiking or exploring. Bears should be warned of your existence, therefore carry bear spray, make noise, and keep your distance.

b. Weather Preparation: The weather in Alaska is unpredictable. Even on bright days, dress in layers and have rain gear nearby. Before leaving, check the weather forecast.

c. Become familiar with the emergency phone numbers for the police, medical help, and other agencies. Call 911 in the US in case of an emergency.

11.4 Packing Checklist

a. Outdoor gear: Bring proper outdoor clothes, hiking boots, rain gear, and bug repellant depending on the season.

b. Binoculars and a camera: Use your camera to capture the breathtaking vistas and animals. Binoculars help see animals and birds.

c. Keep your gadgets charged so they can be used for communication, navigation, and photo-taking.

d. Carrying a reusable water bottle can help you stay hydrated and cut down on trash.

e. Sun protection: To shield yourself from the glare of the sun, don't forget sunglasses, sunscreen, and a wide-brimmed hat.

f. Ensure you have adequate prescription medicine for the length of your trip if you are taking any.

g. Carry a first aid kit that includes the absolute necessities, such as sticky bandages, painkillers, and any personal drugs.

Keep in mind that depending on the season and the activities you want to participate in, your packing list may change. It's a smart idea to do some study on the particular weather and conditions for the dates of your trip.

You'll be ready to make the most of your Homer journey if you keep these useful suggestions in mind. These elements make for a seamless and pleasurable journey, whether you're figuring out how to get about town, interacting with the populace, making sure you're secure, or packing your needs.

11.5 Websites and Apps

Homer Chamber of Commerce: The official website of the Homer Chamber of Commerce offers useful details about places to stay, places to eat, things to do, and events.

a. Learn about Alaska's fishing laws, wildlife-watching advice, and outdoor activities from the Alaska Department of Fish & Game.

b. Find information about Alaska's national parks, forests, and wildlife refuges at the Public Lands Information Centers.

11.6 Useful Contact Details

Homer Visitor Information Center:

Address: 201 Sterling Hwy, Homer, AK 99603
Phone: (907) 235-7740
Email: visitorinfo@homeralaska.org
Emergency Services:

Police, Fire, Medical: 911

11.7 Recommended Reading

a. John McPhee's famous book "Coming into the Country" offers a fascinating look into Alaskan culture and geography, especially the Kenai Peninsula.

b. The book "Two in the Far North" by Margaret E. Murie provides a vivid portrait of Alaska's environment, as well as its flora, animals, and indigenous people.

c. While not explicitly about Alaska, Bill Bryson's witty story of hiking the Appalachian Trail provides amusing insights into the rewards and difficulties of outdoor experiences in "A Walk in the Woods."

d. If you're curious about the local flora, "Wildflowers of Alaska" by Verna Pratt will help you recognize and enjoy the state's wildflowers.

These materials will improve your comprehension of Homer and the history, culture, and natural world of Alaska. These suggestions are a wonderful place to start whether you're searching for useful information or want to immerse yourself in the local tales.

12. Conclusion and Recommendations

In conclusion, Homer, Alaska, provides an exceptional fusion of the outdoors, ethnic diversity, and natural beauty. Every part of this coastal community invites you to experience the true spirit of Alaska, from taking a stroll through Kachemak Bay State Park to indulging in delectable fresh seafood.

The following advice will help you get the most out of your Homer adventure:

a. Immerse yourself in nature by engaging in one of the many available outdoor pursuits, such as fishing excursions, kayaking, hiking, and animal watching. Each encounter fosters a closer relationship with the region's magnificent vistas and diverse animals.

b. Discover Art and Culture: To appreciate the local creative skill, visit Homer's art galleries, such as Fireweed Gallery and Ptarmigan Arts. Visit the Bunnell Street Arts Center for classes and exhibitions if you get the chance.

c. Enjoy the Culinary Delights: Sample the fresh fish at neighborhood eateries like Captain Patties Fish House and The Chart Room to indulge in the abundance of the sea. For a full sense of Homer, investigate the distinctive cuisines of nearby restaurants as well.

d. Attend Local Events: If your visit falls during a gathering like the Kachemak Bay Writers' Conference or the Homer Winter Carnival, make sure to attend. These gatherings provide remarkable experiences and give a glimpse into the culture of the neighborhood.

e. Plan day outings to destinations such as Halibut Cove and Seldovia Village for memorable day adventures that provide a new viewpoint of the region's beauty and way of life.

f. Be Prepared by layering your clothing to account for Alaska's unpredictable weather, carrying bear spray while trekking, and keeping emergency contact information close at hand.

Homer is a place of wonder, adventure, and connection, so never forget that. Your trip to Homer is sure to leave you with treasured memories and a fresh appreciation for the natural world, whether you're attracted to the breathtaking scenery, the innovative arts, or the welcoming community spirit.

Appendix

A. Accommodation Directory

Hotels, Hostels, and Guesthouses:
- Land's End Resort
- Best Western Bidarka Inn
- Homer Inn & Spa

B. Restaurant Guide

Fresh Seafood Restaurants:
- Captain Patties Fish House
- The Chart Room
- Fresh Catch Café

Local Eateries:
- Two Sisters Bakery
- Café Cups
- La Baleine Café

C. Dining Options

To accommodate different tastes and interests, Homer has a broad variety of eating alternatives. You'll find something to please every pallet, from relishing freshly caught fish to indulging in cosmopolitan cuisines.

a. Seafood specialties: Try halibut, salmon, and crab to get a taste of the region's seafood cuisine.

b. International cuisine: Through dishes inspired by French, Mediterranean, and Asian tastes, discover the varied gastronomic scene of Homer.

c. Farm-to-Table: Many meals served at restaurants and cafés use locally sourced, fresh ingredients.

D. Smartphone Photography Tips

a. Capture the Landscape: To capture the expansiveness of Homer's sceneries, from the mountains to the bay, use the panoramic mode.

b. Golden Hour Magic: Use the soft, warm light in the early or late afternoon during the golden hour to take beautiful outdoor pictures.

c. Focus on the features: Take close-up photos of delicate features in nature, such as wildflowers or seashells, using the macro mode on your smartphone.

d. Experiment with taking silhouette photos of people or objects against a bright sky after sunset.

e. HDR option: To balance out high-contrast situations, use the HDR option to make sure that both the bright and dark portions are adequately illuminated.

f. Editing applications: Before sharing your images, improve them by using editing applications to change the lighting, colors, and sharpness.

You now have a convenient resource to further improve your understanding of Homer thanks to the material in the appendix. These tools will enhance your vacation and help you make the most of your stay in this charming Alaskan town, whether you're seeking lodging alternatives, food advice, or smartphone photography advice.

Printed in Great Britain
by Amazon

41403718R00036